It's the Law!
The U.S. Constitution from A to Z
Extended Edition
with the original images of the Declaration of Independence and the U.S. Constitution

by

Joseline Jean-Louis Hardrick

A project of
Twelve:Two Training, LLC

Any Book That Inspires™
A Division of Twelve:Two Training, LLC

It's the Law! The U.S. Consitution from A to Z
Extended Edition
with the original images of the Declaration of Independence and the U.S. Constitution
Written by Joseline J. Hardrick
Illustrated by Teawithami

Original document images courtesy of
The National Archives and Records Administration

Visit my website
www. joselinehardrick.com
and sign up for my mailing list
for free worksheets and
educational resources.

To all the children
who will inherit our democracy.
JJH

- A is for Amendment -
When it's time to make a change
and adjust the Constitution,
we make a new amendment
to avoid any confusion.

- B is for Bill of Rights -
The first ten amendments
that protect the rights of each
to express their freedom
of religion, press, and speech.

- C is for Congress -
It's the legislative branch
which means they make the laws.
They have the power to tax, spend,
and support each cause.

- D is for Declaration of Independence -
Thomas Jefferson wrote it out.
It's a list of resolutions.
The document that started it all,
including the revolution.

- E is for Equal Protection -
It's in the Fourteenth Amendment,
and it has a powerful clause!
We all get certain protections
equally under the laws.

- F is for Freedom -
We have a lot of freedom
and responsibility.
We do what makes us happy,
preserve life and liberty.

- G is for Government -
Both federal and state
are run by public officials.
They each have three branches,
executive, legislative, and judicial.

- H is for House of Representatives -
It's one-half of Congress
and chosen by population.
Each state gets a different amount
so it grows along with the nation.

- I is for Immunities and Privileges -
Benefits and protections
that we all share.
For citizens of this nation,
every state must take care.

- J is for Judicial Branch -
As in the Supreme Court
and every federal judge.
When they interpret specific laws
they usually don't like to budge.

- K is for Kings (and Queens) -
There's no more royalty.
We don't allow them here.
The Constitution bans nobility
to make it very clear.

- L is for Laws -

As in the Constitution,
and statutes, codes, and regulations.
They all make up the set of rules
we must obey throughout the nation.

- M is for Majority Rule -

The majority makes the rule.
At least that's what they say.
When more than 50% say yes (or no)
they're supposed to get their way.

- N is for Naturalization -

To become a citizen
instead of a permanent guest,
you're either born in the U.S.
or swear under oath and take a test.

- O is for Original Intent -
There's lots of debate
about original intent.
Even if the Founders wrote it,
how do we know what they really meant?

- P is for President -

Once Congress passes laws
The President must execute,
give pardons, write orders,
and receive the military salute.

- Q is for Qualifications -
There are many qualifications
to work for the government,
like age and citizenship,
and being a resident.

- R is for Rights -

There are many more rights
than the ones under letter "B."
You have to read between the lines
for dignity and privacy.

- S is for Senate -

The other half of Congress,
they help to make laws too.
They have a lot of power since
each state only gets two.

- T is for Taxes -

Some pay it and some don't,
but we all benefit.
Let's hope they balance it out,
and get rid of the deficit.

- U is for Union -

As a union, we stand,
and that's by design.
All the benefits and burdens
are yours and mine.

- V is for Voting -

Vote every election
for the public good.
Many fought and died so
that every citizen could.

- W is for We the People -
For *women*, *workers*, and
the *worldwide* community.
For all to participate
for the sake of our unity.

- X Marks the Spot -

That's where thirty-nine men
on the dotted line signed
to create this republic,
a new government refined.

- Y is for Yearly Celebration -

America's yearly celebration
is the Fourth of July,
when everyone comes out
to watch fireworks in the sky.

- Z is for Zealous -

Zealous protection
of our right to be free.
Fairness and justice
for all is our guarantee.

Interesting Facts about the U.S. Constitution

The United States went through a lot of changes between the time it issued the Declaration of Independence and the Constitution.
For example, did you know that ...

- The U.S. Constitution was not the first governing document. The U.S. originally had the Articles of Confederation. But it was not working out the way everyone hoped.
- If the Founders did not agree to add a Bill of Rights, the Constitution might not have been ratified.
- The Bill of Rights originally had twelve amendments.

There are a lot more facts about the U.S. Constitution, find out more today by visiting my website, www.joselinehardrick.com, and by following me on social media for updates!

Congress of the United States
begun and held at the City of New-York, on
Wednesday the Fourth of March, one thousand seven hundred and eighty nine
CONGRESS, JULY 4, 1776.
Declaration of the thirteen united States
We the People of the United States,
insure domestic Tranquility, provide for the common defence, promote the general Welfare
and our Posterity, do ordain and establish this Constitution for the United States of America.
Article I

<u>The Declaration of Independence</u>

IN CONGRESS. JULY 4, 1776.

The unanimous Declaration of the thirteen united States of America.

This image is of the actual Declaration of Independence parchment.

The faded condition of the parchment of the Declaration of Independence is due to years of public display. When the National Archives removed the Declaration of Independence from the Rotunda in 2001 to prepare it for a new case, it inspected the reverse side. No treasure map was found, but there was one line of text, "The Original Declaration of Independence July 4th 1776," at the bottom.

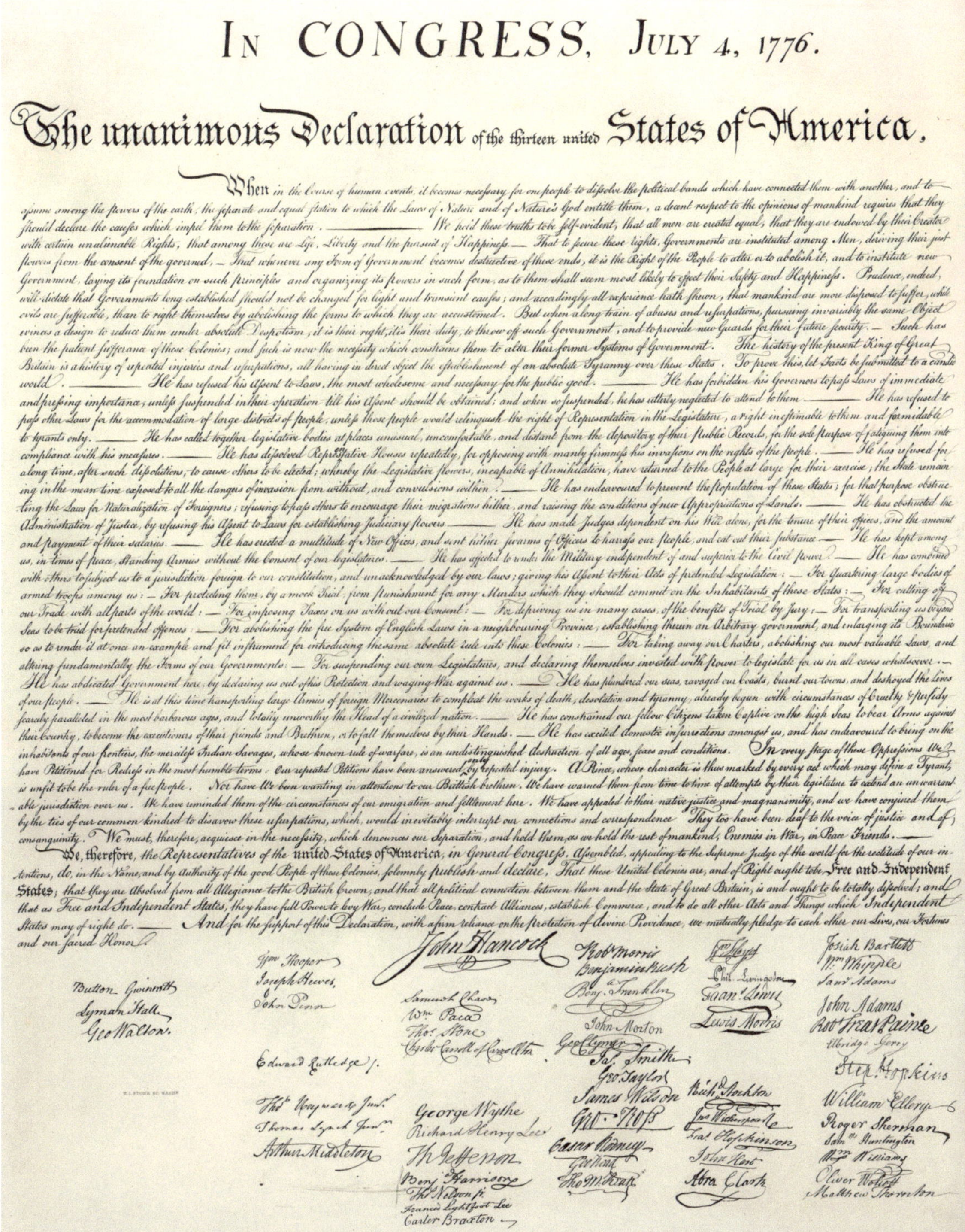

IN CONGRESS, JULY 4, 1776.

The unanimous Declaration of the thirteen united States of America,

When in the Course of human events, it becomes necessary for one people to dissolve the political bands which have connected them with another, and to assume among the powers of the earth, the separate and equal station to which the Laws of Nature and of Nature's God entitle them, a decent respect to the opinions of mankind requires that they should declare the causes which impel them to the separation. — We hold these truths to be self-evident, that all men are created equal, that they are endowed by their Creator with certain unalienable Rights, that among these are Life, Liberty and the pursuit of Happiness. — That to secure these rights, Governments are instituted among Men, deriving their just powers from the consent of the governed, — That whenever any Form of Government becomes destructive of these ends, it is the Right of the People to alter or to abolish it, and to institute new Government, laying its foundation on such principles and organizing its powers in such form, as to them shall seem most likely to effect their Safety and Happiness. Prudence, indeed, will dictate that Governments long established should not be changed for light and transient causes; and accordingly all experience hath shewn, that mankind are more disposed to suffer, while evils are sufferable, than to right themselves by abolishing the forms to which they are accustomed. But when a long train of abuses and usurpations, pursuing invariably the same Object evinces a design to reduce them under absolute Despotism, it is their right, it is their duty, to throw off such Government, and to provide new Guards for their future security. — Such has been the patient sufferance of these Colonies; and such is now the necessity which constrains them to alter their former Systems of Government. The history of the present King of Great Britain is a history of repeated injuries and usurpations, all having in direct object the establishment of an absolute Tyranny over these States. To prove this, let Facts be submitted to a candid world. — He has refused his Assent to Laws, the most wholesome and necessary for the public good. — He has forbidden his Governors to pass Laws of immediate and pressing importance, unless suspended in their operation till his Assent should be obtained; and when so suspended, he has utterly neglected to attend to them. — He has refused to pass other Laws for the accommodation of large districts of people, unless those people would relinquish the right of Representation in the Legislature, a right inestimable to them and formidable to tyrants only. — He has called together legislative bodies at places unusual, uncomfortable, and distant from the depository of their Public Records, for the sole purpose of fatiguing them into compliance with his measures. — He has dissolved Representative Houses repeatedly, for opposing with manly firmness his invasions on the rights of the people. — He has refused for a long time, after such dissolutions, to cause others to be elected; whereby the Legislative powers, incapable of Annihilation, have returned to the People at large for their exercise; the State remaining in the mean time exposed to all the dangers of invasion from without, and convulsions within. — He has endeavoured to prevent the population of these States; for that purpose obstructing the Laws for Naturalization of Foreigners; refusing to pass others to encourage their migrations hither, and raising the conditions of new Appropriations of Lands. — He has obstructed the Administration of Justice, by refusing his Assent to Laws for establishing Judiciary powers. — He has made Judges dependent on his Will alone, for the tenure of their offices, and the amount and payment of their salaries. — He has erected a multitude of New Offices, and sent hither swarms of Officers to harrass our people, and eat out their substance. — He has kept among us, in times of peace, Standing Armies without the Consent of our legislatures. — He has affected to render the Military independent of and superior to the Civil power. — He has combined with others to subject us to a jurisdiction foreign to our constitution, and unacknowledged by our laws; giving his Assent to their Acts of pretended Legislation: — For Quartering large bodies of armed troops among us: — For protecting them, by a mock Trial, from punishment for any Murders which they should commit on the Inhabitants of these States: — For cutting off our Trade with all parts of the world: — For imposing Taxes on us without our Consent: — For depriving us in many cases, of the benefits of Trial by Jury: — For transporting us beyond Seas to be tried for pretended offences: — For abolishing the free System of English Laws in a neighbouring Province, establishing therein an Arbitrary government, and enlarging its Boundaries so as to render it at once an example and fit instrument for introducing the same absolute rule into these Colonies: — For taking away our Charters, abolishing our most valuable Laws, and altering fundamentally the Forms of our Governments: — For suspending our own Legislatures, and declaring themselves invested with power to legislate for us in all cases whatsoever. — He has abdicated Government here, by declaring us out of his Protection and waging War against us. — He has plundered our seas, ravaged our Coasts, burnt our towns, and destroyed the lives of our people. — He is at this time transporting large Armies of foreign Mercenaries to compleat the works of death, desolation and tyranny, already begun with circumstances of Cruelty & perfidy scarcely paralleled in the most barbarous ages, and totally unworthy the Head of a civilized nation. — He has constrained our fellow Citizens taken Captive on the high Seas to bear Arms against their Country, to become the executioners of their friends and Brethren, or to fall themselves by their Hands. — He has excited domestic insurrections amongst us, and has endeavoured to bring on the inhabitants of our frontiers, the merciless Indian Savages, whose known rule of warfare, is an undistinguished destruction of all ages, sexes and conditions. In every stage of these Oppressions We have Petitioned for Redress in the most humble terms: Our repeated Petitions have been answered only by repeated injury. A Prince, whose character is thus marked by every act which may define a Tyrant, is unfit to be the ruler of a free people. Nor have We been wanting in attentions to our British brethren. We have warned them from time to time of attempts by their legislature to extend an unwarrantable jurisdiction over us. We have reminded them of the circumstances of our emigration and settlement here. We have appealed to their native justice and magnanimity, and we have conjured them by the ties of our common kindred to disavow these usurpations, which, would inevitably interrupt our connections and correspondence. They too have been deaf to the voice of justice and of consanguinity. We must, therefore, acquiesce in the necessity, which denounces our Separation, and hold them, as we hold the rest of mankind, Enemies in War, in Peace Friends. —

We, therefore, the Representatives of the united States of America, in General Congress, Assembled, appealing to the Supreme Judge of the world for the rectitude of our intentions, do, in the Name, and by Authority of the good People of these Colonies, solemnly publish and declare, That these United Colonies are, and of Right ought to be Free and Independent States; that they are Absolved from all Allegiance to the British Crown, and that all political connection between them and the State of Great Britain, is and ought to be totally dissolved; and that as Free and Independent States, they have full Power to levy War, conclude Peace, contract Alliances, establish Commerce, and to do all other Acts and Things which Independent States may of right do. — And for the support of this Declaration, with a firm reliance on the protection of divine Providence, we mutually pledge to each other our Lives, our Fortunes and our sacred Honor.

John Hancock

Button Gwinnett, Lyman Hall, Geo Walton.

Wm Hooper, Joseph Hewes, John Penn

Edward Rutledge, Thos Heyward Junr, Thomas Lynch Junr, Arthur Middleton

Samuel Chase, Wm Paca, Thos Stone, Charles Carroll of Carrollton

George Wythe, Richard Henry Lee, Th Jefferson, Benja Harrison, Thos Nelson jr, Francis Lightfoot Lee, Carter Braxton

Robt Morris, Benjamin Rush, Benja Franklin, John Morton, Geo Clymer, Jas Smith, Geo Taylor, James Wilson, Geo Ross

Caesar Rodney, Geo Read, Thos M:Kean

Wm Floyd, Phil Livingston, Frans Lewis, Lewis Morris

Richd Stockton, Jno Witherspoon, Fras Hopkinson, John Hart, Abra Clark

Josiah Bartlett, Wm Whipple, Saml Adams, John Adams, Robt Treat Paine, Elbridge Gerry, Step Hopkins, William Ellery, Roger Sherman, Sam el Huntington, Wm Williams, Oliver Wolcott, Matthew Thornton

This image is of the frequently reproduced 1823 engraving by William J. Stone.

In 1820, the Declaration of Independence was already fading. Secretary of State John Quincy Adams hired printer William J. Stone to make a full-size copperplate engraving. This plate was used to print copies of the Declaration. The 1823 Stone engraving is the most frequently reproduced version of the Declaration.

The U.S. Constitution

We the People

Article. I

According to the National Archives:

"The Constitution acted like a colossal merger, uniting a group of states with different interests, laws, and cultures. "

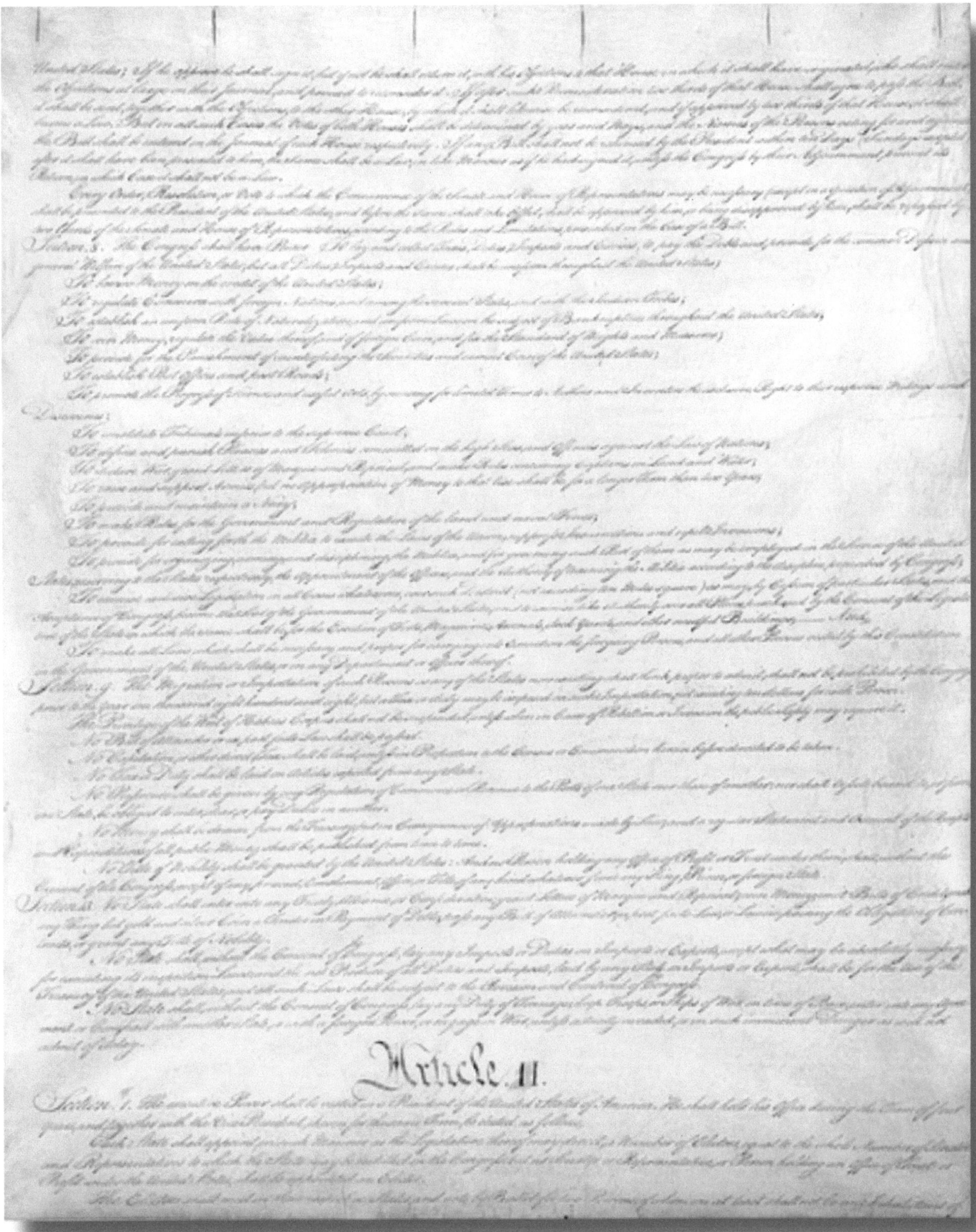
Article. II.

"Under America's first national government, the Articles of Confederation, the states acted together only for specific purposes."

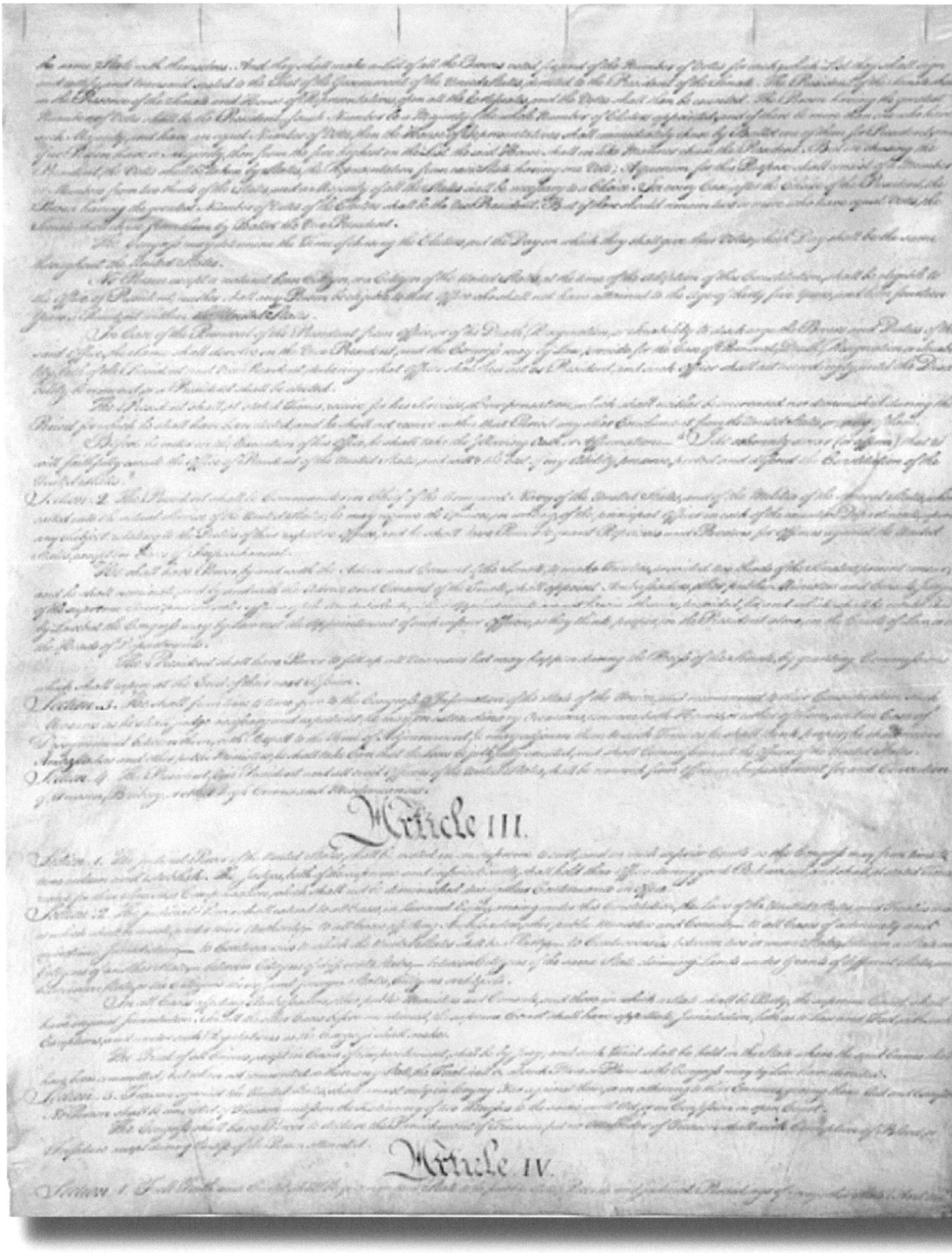

Article III.

Article IV.

"The Constitution united its citizens as members of a whole, vesting the power of the union in the people. "

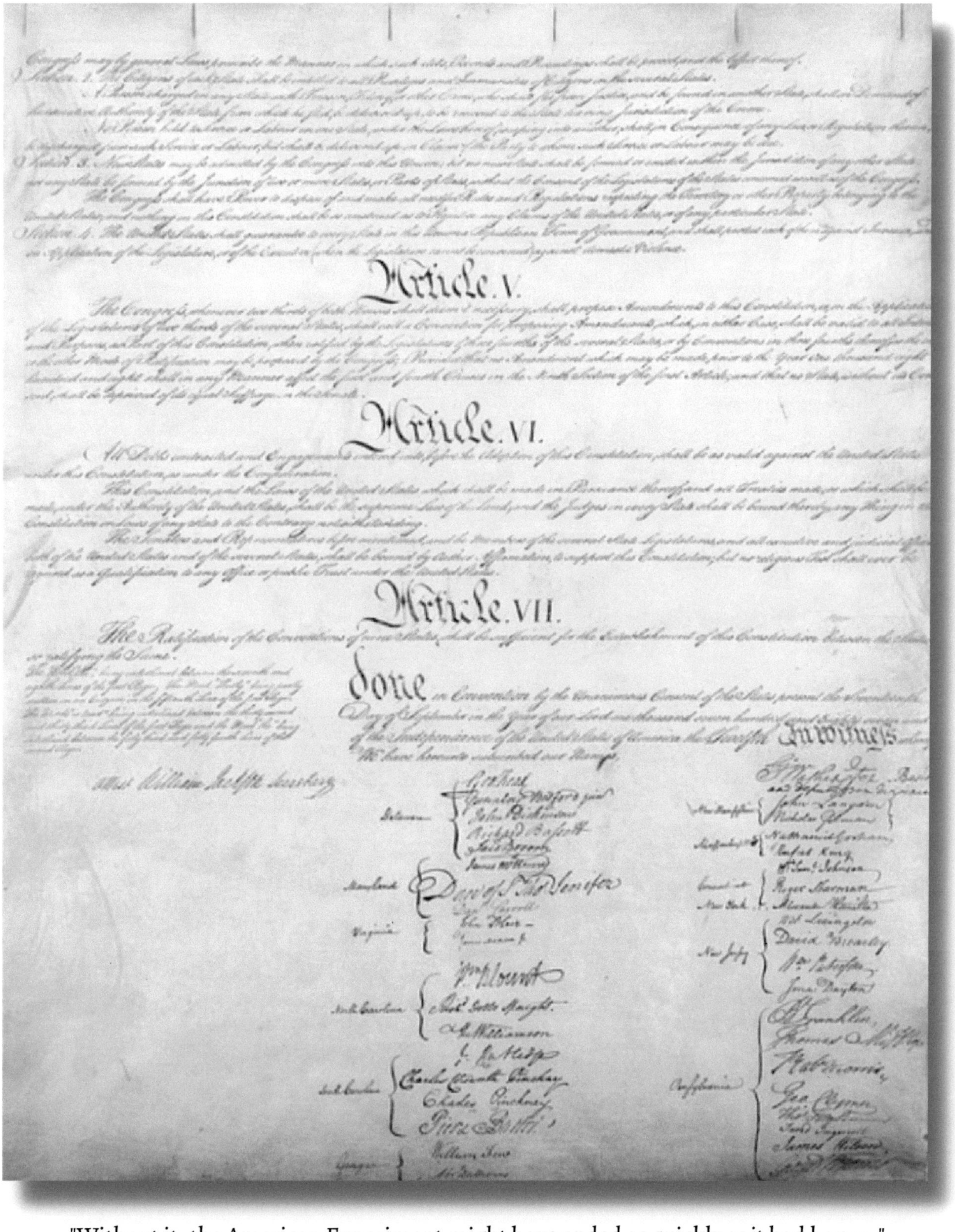
Article. V.

Article. VI.

Article. VII.

"Without it, the American Experiment might have ended as quickly as it had begun."
https://www.archives.gov/founding-docs/constitution

All four pages of the document are on permanent display at the National Archives.

The Bill of Rights

Congress of the United States,

THE

RESOLVED

ARTICLES

The first ten amendments to the Constitution gave citizens more confidence in the new government and contain many of America's most valued freedoms.
https://www.archives.gov/founding-docs/bill-of-rights

Joseline J. Hardrick

I love reading children's books. When I taught elementary school many years ago, my favorite part of the day was reading to the kids. Now that I have my own son, Little George, I have read many more books and have been inspired to write my own. My son was not impressed with the first one I wrote, so I kept trying until he laughed aloud while I read it.

So began my journey as a children's book author. And now Little George has joined me in writing some of the books; from story ideas to illustrations, we worked together to create fun stories for young kids.

I hope your child enjoys this book as much as I enjoyed making it. Please consider leaving a review on Amazon.com. Visit my website at www.joselinehardrick.com or by scanning the QR code for free activity worksheets.

Made in the USA
Monee, IL
19 October 2026

66036202R00026